From Laught to Latkes

A Joyful Journey Through Jewish Cooking and Comedy

Published by MARKANDMARKSCO LIMITED © 2023

Introduction

We're delighted that, through whatever means, this book has found its way to you. It will take you on a culinary and comedic journey through the Jewish experience, bringing together two of the enduring legacies that Jews have given to the world, its cuisine, and its humour.

From the simmering pans of matzo ball soup to the raucous and boisterous tales shared around the Sabbath table, Jewish cuisine and humour are a wonderful, intertwined dance that tell the story of perseverance and adaptability, culture and tradition.

When people think of Jewish food, what most often springs to mind is the world-famous bagel. These gorgeous, chewy, ring-shaped bread rolls are synonymous with Jewish tradition and culture. Add a big dollop of cream cheese and smoked salmon and you have one of the most iconic and universally recognised Jewish foods.

Jewish cuisine, however, is a rich and diverse tapestry that brings together centuries of history, migration and different cultural influences, evolving over time, and reflecting the experiences and traditions of Jewish communities throughout the world.

Ashkenazi Jews who settled in Eastern Europe brought with them the culinary traditions of that region, giving rise to notable and famous dishes such as chicken matzo ball soup and gefilte fish. Sephardic Jews, who originally hailed from the Iberian Peninsula and later, migrated to North Africa and the Middle East, brought with them dishes known for their vibrant spices and aromatic herbs.

There has been a resurgence of interest in Jewish cuisine in recent years led by some renowned and talented chefs. This culinary revival has led to the rediscovering, reinventing and reinterpreting of traditional classic recipes and an increasing appreciation for the depth and complexity of Jewish ingredients and flavours. At work in this resurgence is a continuous interplay between tradition and innovation.

Jewish humour and indeed, the tradition of humour in Judaism, dates back centuries to the Torah and the Midrash from the ancient Middle East. It is shaped by the unique experiences of the Jewish people.

'Chutzpah', a Yiddish term meaning audacity or nerve, is a key element of Jewish humour, reflecting the confidence and self-assurance with which Jewish comedians throughout history have tackled difficult subjects, using it to help turn adversity into laughter.

Good Jewish jokes do more than make you laugh, they illuminate the intricate and complex corners of Jewish psyche, culture, and history. Having squabbles is in the very DNA of being Jewish. Most cultures only complain when there's something to complain about, but in Jewish culture, and in its humour especially, we see that you can also express contentment by means of a complaint.

Kvetching (a Yiddish word for complaining), a staple of Jewish jokes, becomes a way of exerting control over a hostile universe, penetrating to the heart of the Ashkenazi Jewish mindset. When things are going well, Jews think of them as a little bit bad, and when things aren't going well, Jews try to make it a little better through humour. That is quintessentially a Jewish perspective.

Some Jewish jokes capture an essential truth, that as Jews, we are a little obstreperous by nature; some help to keep Judaism alive at all costs; while others are not just jokes, more like short stories, doing as we have always done with our history, passing stories down through the generations. Our jokes don't hurt anyone, they unite people.

Jewish humour stands a s testament to the resilience and creative spirit of its people. Its enduring legacy and significance is its ability to find humour in the face of adversity and bring people together, through laughter. When Jews crack jokes about themselves, it's a unique blend of poking fun and expressing love. Every part of the world has its humour, Jews just happen to have the best!

Before we get started………….

What's the difference between a Jewish pessimist and a Jewish optimist?

The Jewish pessimist says, "Things can't possibly get any worse."

The Jewish optimist says, "Sure they can!"

Enjoy the recipes and ensure you have a laugh along the way.

What's cooking?

STARTERS
Chicken Noodle Soup with Kneidlach
Borscht
Simple Chopped Liver Pâté
Gefilte Fish
Chopped Herring
Israeli Salad
Potato Latkes
Hummus
Savoury Potato Kugel
Challah Bread

MAINS
Shakshuka
Matzo Brei
Simple Salt Beef
Simple Falafel
Israeli-Style Fish Cakes
Jewish Style Brisket
Chicken Schnitzel
Classic Jewish smoked salmon and cream cheese bagel
Baked Salmon with Herb Tahini Sauce

DESERTS
Cheese Blintzes with Cherry
Chocolate Babka Cake
Jewish Apple Cake
Honey Cake
Sweet Kugel
Sufganiyot

STARTERS

Chicken Noodle Soup with Kneidlach

Generations of Jewish mothers and grandmothers have sworn by the healing properties of Jewish Penicillin - chicken noodle soup with matzo balls (kneidlach) - touting its healing properties for everything from a cold to a broken heart.

Ingredients:

1 whole chicken (approx. 1.5kg), or chicken parts
3 large carrots, peeled and cut into large chunks
3 celery stalks, cut into large chunks
2 large onions, quartered
1 small bunch of fresh parsley
1 small bunch of fresh dill
1 teaspoon whole black peppercorns
Salt, to taste
Water
Matzo balls and/or egg noodles (optional)

Instructions:

Place the chicken in a large pot. If using a whole chicken, you may want to cut it into pieces to allow it to fit better.

Add the carrots, celery, onions, parsnip (if using), parsley, dill, peppercorns, and a generous pinch of salt.

Add enough water to the pot to cover the ingredients by an inch or two. The amount will vary depending on the size of your pot but is usually about 12-16 cups.

Bring the water to a boil over medium-high heat. Once boiling, reduce the heat to low and let the soup simmer.

As the soup simmers, skim off any foam or impurities that rise to the top. This will help keep the broth clear.

Continue to simmer the soup, partially covered, for about 2-3 hours.

After the soup has simmered, strain it through a fine-mesh sieve or cheesecloth. Be sure to save the carrots and chicken, discarding the rest of the solids. You can shred the chicken and add it back to the soup and slice the carrots.

If you're adding matzo balls or egg noodles, cook them according to their respective recipes or package instructions, then add them to the soup. Season the soup with additional salt, if needed, and serve.

The Kneidlach

Ingredients:

3 eggs
5 Tbsp melted fat (cooled)
½ cup of water
1 cup matzo meal
1 tsp of salt and pepper

Instructions:

Whisk the eggs until very frothy.

Whisk in the water, then the fat.

Add the matzo meal, stirring until it starts to thicken.

Leave for at least 2 hours (or longer)

Form into balls and cook in boiling water for 30 minutes

Can be cooked ahead of time and reheated

Nervous Waiter

A group of five Jewish women are eating lunch in a busy cafe.

Nervously, their waiter approaches the table.

"Ladies," he says.

"Is anything okay?"

Borscht

Borscht is a traditional Eastern European soup made primarily from beetroot, thus giving the soup its distinctive red colour. Depending on the region there can be many variations of this soup, some made with meat or bone broth, and others which are vegetarian. Here's a basic recipe but feel free to experiment.

Ingredients:

2 good sized beetroots, peeled and grated, 1 large carrot, peeled and grated
1 medium onion, chopped, 2 big or 3 small cloves of garlic, minced
2 tablespoons vegetable oil
1 ltr or 4 cups vegetable stock or beef/bone broth
1 medium potato, peeled and diced
1/2 head of purple cabbage, thinly sliced (regular cabbage will do)
2-3 tablespoons tomato paste
2 tablespoons of lemon juice, salt and pepper to taste
Fresh dill and sour cream for serving

Instructions:

Heat the vegetable oil in a large pot over a medium heat. Add the onion, carrot, and beetroots. Cook for approximately 10 minutes, until the vegetables are softened. Add the garlic and cook for another minute.
Add the tomato paste to the pot and stir well. Cook for another 2-3 minutes.
Pour in the vegetable stock or beef broth, add the diced potato, and bring the mixture to a boil. Then reduce the heat to low, cover the pot, and simmer until the potato is tender, about 15 minutes.
Add the sliced cabbage to the pot and cook until the cabbage is tender, about 10 more minutes.
Stir in the lemon juice, and season with salt and pepper. Let it simmer for a couple of more minutes. Serve hot, topped with a dollop of sour cream and a sprinkle of fresh dill.

Experiment to find the version that you like best, remembering that borscht is flexible and can be adjusted to suit your taste. Some versions even include beans, tomatoes or peppers. Enjoy!

Taste the Borscht

Every day, Morrie has lunch in the same deli, and every day Morrie orders the borscht soup.

One day he gets his soup, and as the waiter starts walking away, Morrie says, "Come back, please, taste the borscht."

"What's wrong, Morrie?"
"Taste the borscht."
"What's the problem?"
"Taste the borscht."

"You've had that soup every day for 35 years. If there's a problem, just tell me?"

"Taste. The. Borscht."
"Is it too salty? Is there a fly in it, G-d forbid?"
"Taste the Borscht!"
"Okay, fine. I'll taste the Borscht. Where's the spoon?"
"Aha!"

Simple Chopped Liver Pâté

This popular Ashkenazi Jewish appetizer is a staple menu item in Jewish delis and restaurants, and often served as part of a traditional Sabbath Friday night dinner.

Ingredients:

3/4 kg of chicken livers
2 large onions, finely chopped
2 cloves garlic, minced
60ml (1/4 cup) of schmaltz (chicken fat). Substituted with butter but not as good!
3 hard-boiled eggs
Salt and freshly ground pepper to taste
Fresh parsley for garnish (optional)

Instructions:

Trim the livers for any excess fat or sinew. Rinse and pat them dry.
In a large pan, heat 2 tablespoons of the schmaltz (or butter) over medium heat. Add the onions and cook until they become translucent (5-7 minutes).
Add the garlic and cook for another minute.
Increase the heat to medium-high and add the chicken livers. Cook until browned but still slightly pink in the centre (approximately 2-3 minutes per side).
Try not to overcook the livers or they will become tough. Remove the pan from the heat and let it cool slightly. Transfer the liver mixture to a food processor.
Add the hard-boiled eggs, remaining 2 tablespoons of schmaltz or butter, salt, and pepper. Process until the mixture is smooth, stopping to scrape down the sides as needed.
Taste and adjust the seasoning if needed. Garnish with some parsley or some additional grated boiled egg.
Transfer the pâté to a serving bowl, cover, and refrigerate for at least 2 hours, or until firm. Delicious with rye bread, challah bread or matzo.

Rowing Crew

A yeshiva decides to start a rowing team. But no matter how much they practice, they lose every race they enter.

Eventually the team decides to send one boy down to the nearby rowing club as a spy, to watch their winning crew team and find out what their secret is.

After a couple of days of reconnaissance, the boy comes back. "Listen!" he tells his teammates. "I learned how they do it — they have eight guys rowing, and only one guy screaming!"

Potato Latkes

Potato latkes are closely associated with the Jewish holiday of Hanukkah. This simple traditional recipe should make about 12 latkes.

Ingredients:

1kg of russet potatoes
1 large onion
2 large eggs
1/2 cup all-purpose flour
1 teaspoon salt
1/2 teaspoon black pepper
Vegetable oil, for frying
Applesauce, for serving (optional)
Sour cream, for serving (optional)

Instructions:

Peel the potatoes and the onion. Using a food processor with a grating blade or a box grater, grate the potatoes and the onion.
Transfer the grated potatoes and onion to a clean dish towel. Wrap them in the towel and wring out as much excess liquid as you can. This step is crucial for getting the latkes to be crispy.
Transfer the potato and onion mixture to a large bowl. Add the eggs, flour, salt, and pepper, then stir until the flour is absorbed.
In a large flying pan over medium-high heat, heat a thin layer of oil.
Use a tablespoon scoop of the mixture to create discs and drop them into the pan. Cook until they're golden and crispy on both sides, about 5 minutes per side.
Transfer the latkes to a paper towel-lined plate to drain and cool slightly. Repeat with the remaining batter, adding more oil to the pan as needed.
Serve the latkes warm (and fresh if possible) with applesauce and/or sour cream, if desired. (Some Jewish households sprinkle a little sugar on their latkes).

Remember, you can also adjust the size of your latkes to suit your personal preference.

The New Ruth

Ruth Greenberg has a heart attack and is rushed to hospital. While she's in the emergency room, her heart stops and her soul leaves her body. Ruth appears before G-d and asks, "G-d, is that it, I'm only 56?" G-d answers, "No, Ruth, you have another 30 great years. Go and enjoy your life."

Back in the emergency room, the doctors work their magic, the electric shocks work and Ruth comes back to life. She's thrilled by her new lease on life. So, while she's in hospital, she decides to make the most of it.

She does the lot, tummy tuck, neck lift, liposuction, facelift, nose job, breast enlargement, buttock enhancement, the full works. The day before she leaves hospital, she brings in the hair stylist, a beautician, and fashion consultant for a total makeover.

When Ruth finally leaves the hospital, she looks incredible. She steps out into the street, and bang! She gets hit by an ambulance and dies instantly. Her soul goes back to heaven and again she comes before G-d.

She says, "G-d, what happened? You told me I had another 30 years. Why didn't you save me?"
"Ruth!" G-d says, "I didn't recognize you."

Gefilte Fish

Gefilte Fish is an iconic Ashkenazi Jewish dish, consisting of poached fish balls made from a mixture of ground deboned fish, onions, and various seasonings. Gefilte fish can be an acquired taste for some, especially those unfamiliar with traditional Ashkenazi Jewish dishes.

Ingredients:

1kg of mixed fish filets (such as carp, whitefish, pike), skinned and deboned
1 large onion, finely chopped
2 eggs
1/4 cup matzah meal (breadcrumbs will do but matzah meal is best)
1 tablespoon sugar to taste
1 teaspoon salt
1/2 teaspoon ground white or black pepper
1 cup of cold water or fish stock

For the Poaching Liquid:

1 onion, 1 carrot, sliced
2 cups fish stock or water
Salt and pepper to taste
A few sprigs of fresh dill (optional)

Instructions:

In a large bowl, combine the ground fish, chopped onion, eggs, matzah meal or breadcrumbs, sugar, salt, pepper, and water or fish stock.

Mix well until everything is thoroughly combined.

Form Balls: With wet hands (this prevents the mixture from sticking), take some of the fish mixture and shape it into oval balls or patties.

To prepare the poaching liquid: in a large pot, add slices of onion, carrot, fish stock or water, and season with salt and pepper.

Bring it to a simmer.

Gently place the fish balls/patties into the simmering poaching liquid.

If you're using dill, you can add some sprigs for additional flavour.

Cover the pot and let them simmer for about 30-45 minutes.

Once cooked, remove the gefilte fish with a slotted spoon and place them in a dish.

Strain the poaching liquid over the fish, ensuring that each serving has a slice of carrot.

Let the gefilte fish cool down, then refrigerate.

Jewish Mother

A Jewish woman is elected president of the United States.

As the inauguration approaches, she says to her mother, "Mum, you've got to come.

"The mother says, "Sure, I'll go, but what am I going to wear? It's outdoors, it's freezing cold.

 Why did you have to run for president? What kind of job is that? You'll have nothing but problems."

But she goes to the inauguration, and just as her daughter is being sworn in by the chief justice, the mother turns to the senator next to her and says,

"You see that girl up there? Her brother's a doctor."

Israeli Salad

Israeli salad is best known for its very finely chopped fresh ingredients. It's a refreshing side dish that pairs wonderfully with many meals. It is often enjoyed for breakfast in Israel, alongside olives, cheese, and bread.

Ingredients:

4 good-sized tomatoes, finely diced
4 good-sized cucumbers, finely diced
1 medium red onion, finely diced (optional)
1 pepper (red, yellow, or green), finely diced
2-3 tablespoons fresh parsley, finely chopped
2-3 tablespoons fresh mint, finely chopped (optional)
2-3 tablespoons olive oil
1-2 tablespoons fresh lemon juice
Salt and pepper, to taste

Instructions:

Wash and prep all the salad items.

Finely dice the tomatoes, cucumbers, pepper, and red onion. (Remember, the characteristic of Israeli salad is that the ingredients are very finely chopped).

In a large bowl, combine the diced tomatoes, cucumbers, pepper, and onion. Add the chopped parsley and mint to the mix.

Drizzle the olive oil and fresh lemon juice over the vegetables. Season with salt and pepper.

Gently toss all the ingredients until well mixed. Adjust seasoning if necessary. For added flavor, you could also add a touch of sumac or za'atar.

Serve immediately or refrigerate to let the flavors meld together. It's best served chilled.

The Rabbi and the Cabbie

A rabbi and a cab driver are in line to get into heaven. The rabbi, a man of G-d, is sure he'll get in. The cab driver is a little nervous.

When they reach heaven's gate, they both get in and the cab driver breathes a sigh of relief. It's time for them to be shown where they'll be living.

The rabbi is shown to a very nice apartment in a nice building on a beautiful street. He walks out on his balcony and is astonished to see the cab driver being shown into a big, fully-staffed, gorgeous mansion on a hill with an incredible view.

The rabbi calls the front desk of heaven and says, "I'm not the complaining type, my place is very nice, but I dedicated my whole life to bringing my congregations closer to G-d, yet the cab driver gets the beautiful mansion on the hill. What's going on?"

The front desk tells him, "To be honest, Rabbi, when you were lecturing to your congregations, most people were asleep. But when that cabbie was driving, everybody was praying!"

Chopped Herring

Chopped Herring is another traditional Ashkenazi Jewish dish, made from pickled herring, onions, and sometimes apples. It was often a staple at Shabbat tables, especially among poorer families, as herring was an inexpensive source of protein.

Ingredients:

8-10 pickled herring filets (often available in jars at supermarkets or delis)
1 onion, coarsely chopped
1 tart apple (like Granny Smith), peeled, cored, and coarsely chopped
2 hard-boiled eggs
1 tablespoon sugar - to taste
1 tablespoon vinegar (preferably white or apple cider)
2 tablespoons sour cream or mayonnaise (optional, for creaminess)
Freshly ground black pepper, to taste
Fresh dill for garnish (optional)

Instructions

Using a food processor (by hand with a knife is also ok), coarsely chop the herring filets. Place them in a large mixing bowl. (If the pickled herring is particularly salty, you might want to soak them in water for an hour or two, then drain).
In the food processor, chop the onion and apple until they are finely minced. Add these to the bowl with the herring.
Coarsely chop the hard-boiled eggs and add them to the bowl.
To the herring, onion, apple, and eggs, add sugar, vinegar, and freshly ground black pepper. Mix well. (For a creamier texture, you can add sour cream or mayonnaise). Adjust seasoning to taste.
Transfer the chopped herring to a serving dish, cover, and refrigerate for a few hours to let the flavors combine. Before serving, garnish with fresh dill if desired.

Chopped herring is best served on rye bread, crackers, or challah bread.

Abe's Final Words

Elderly Abe Greenberg is lying on his deathbed.

"Is my wife Abigail here?" he asks. "Yes," says Abigail. "I'm here with you!" "Are my children here?" "Yes, Abe, all your children are all here," "Are my grandchildren here?" "Yes, all of the grandchildren are here. Abe, the whole family is here with you!"

Abe Greenberg lifts his head one last time, opens his eyes, and asks, "So why is the light on in the kitchen?"

Challah Bread

Challah is a traditional Jewish bread closely associated with the Sabbath and Jewish holidays. Its braided design is symbolic, with some interpretations linking the braided strands to love, truth, and peace.

Ingredients:

1 1/2 cups warm water (about 45°C/110°F)
2 tablespoons active dry yeast
1/2 cup honey
1/2 cup olive oil (or melted butter)
5 large eggs (4 for the dough and 1 for brushing)
1 tablespoon salt
8-9 cups all-purpose flour

Instructions:

In a large mixing bowl, combine warm water, yeast, and a teaspoon of honey. Let it sit for about 10 minutes until it becomes frothy. To the yeast mixture, add the remaining honey, olive oil (or butter), 4 beaten eggs, and salt. Mix well. Gradually add flour to the mixture, one cup at a time, mixing continuously until the dough begins to come together. Once the dough has formed, transfer it to a floured surface and knead for about 10 minutes, or until it's smooth and elastic.
Place the kneaded dough in a large, oiled bowl, cover with a damp cloth, and let it rise in a warm spot for 1-2 hours, or until it has doubled in size.
After the first rise, push down the dough to release air bubbles. Divide the dough based on how many strands you want for your braid. Roll each portion into long ropes and braid them together. Place the braided loaf on a baking sheet lined with parchment paper. Cover it with a damp cloth and let it rise again for about 45 minutes to an hour.
While the dough is rising, preheat your oven to 190°C / 375°F. Beat the remaining egg and brush it over the surface of the braided loaf. This will give the challah a beautiful shiny brown finish when baked.
Bake in the preheated oven for about 25-35 minutes, or until the challah sounds hollow when tapped on the bottom and place it on a wire rack to cool.

Ham Sandwich

A rabbi and a priest are sitting next to each other on a long-distance flight, and they start chatting.

Having gotten to know each other, after a couple of hours, the priest says to the rabbi, "Rabbi, I hope you won't mind me asking, have you ever succumbed to temptation and tried a little pork?"

The rabbi says, "You know Father, I must confess. I was so curious about it that I did once try a ham sandwich."

A little while later the rabbi felt comfortable enough to ask the priest, "Father, tell me, in all your years, did you ever succumb to temptation and see what it was like to be with a woman?"

The priest says, "Rabbi, I'm going to be honest with you. Yes, one time I gave in and experienced the joys of the flesh."

"So, Father," the rabbi replies, "it beats the heck out of a ham sandwich, doesn't it?"

Hummus

Hummus is a creamy blend of chickpeas, tahini, lemon, and garlic that has been gracing plates for centuries. The word itself is an Arabic term that simply means, 'chickpeas.'

Ingredients:

1 can (15 oz) chickpeas or about 1.5 cups cooked chickpeas
juice of one fresh, large lemon
1/4 cup tahini (well-stirred before measuring)
1-2 minced garlic cloves
2 tablespoons extra virgin olive oil (plus more for serving)
1/2 teaspoon ground cumin
Salt to taste
2 to 3 tablespoons water or as needed for desired consistency
Paprika, for serving (optional)

Instructions:

In a food processor, combine the tahini and lemon juice. Process for 1 minute. Scrape down the sides and process for 30 more seconds.
Add the olive oil, minced garlic, cumin, and a 1/2 teaspoon of salt to the whipped tahini and lemon juice. Process for 30 seconds, scrape down the sides, and process for another 30 seconds.
Drain and rinse the chickpeas. Add half of the chickpeas to the food processor and process for 1 minute. Scrape down the sides of the bowl, add the remaining chickpeas, and process for 1-2 minutes or until thick and quite smooth.
The hummus will most likely be too thick or still have tiny bits of chickpea. To fix this, with the food processor turned on, slowly add 2 to 3 tablespoons of water until you achieve your required consistency.
Transfer the hummus to a bowl and create a shallow well in the center. Drizzle with extra virgin olive oil and sprinkle with paprika if desired.
Store hummus covered in the refrigerator for up to one week. (Before serving after refrigeration, you may want to stir in a little bit of water to help regain the smooth and creamy texture).

Bar Mitzvahs

A synagogue has a big mice problem.

The caretaker tries bait, traps, poison, everything.

Nothing works.

Finally, he goes to the rabbi and explains the problem.

"I have the solution," the rabbi says. "What?" says the caretaker. "It's a foolproof plan," the rabbi says, smiling. "I'll give them all Bar Mitzvahs — we'll never see them again!"

MAINS

Shakshuka

Shakshuka is a traditional dish that consists of poached eggs in a sauce of tomatoes, chilli peppers, and onions, often spiced with cumin. While widely popular in Israeli cuisine and often associated with breakfast, its roots trace back to North Africa. The name "Shakshuka" is of Berber origin, meaning "a mixture". Now, here's the fun part: if you ever oversleep and miss breakfast, don't worry!

Ingredients:

2 tablespoons olive oil
1 large onion, chopped
1 red pepper, chopped
2 cloves garlic, minced
1 teaspoon cumin
1 teaspoon paprika
1/4 teaspoon cayenne pepper (optional, for heat)
1 can diced tomatoes
Salt and pepper to taste
5-6 eggs
Fresh parsley, chopped for garnish
Crumbled feta cheese (optional)

Instructions:

Heat the olive oil in a large frying pan over medium heat.

Add the chopped onion and red pepper to the pan and sauté until they are softened, about 5 minutes.

Add the minced garlic, cumin, paprika, and cayenne pepper (if using) to the pan, and sauté for another 1-2 minutes until the garlic is fragrant and the spices are well mixed in.

Pour in the diced tomatoes with their juice. Season with salt and pepper, then stir everything together.

Reduce the heat to low, cover the pan, and let the mixture simmer for about 15 minutes.

After 15 minutes, create small wells in the tomato mixture for each egg.

Crack an egg into each well.

Cover the pan and let the eggs cook until they are done to your liking.

This will take about 5-7 minutes for runny yolks, or longer for more fully cooked eggs.

Remove the pan from the heat. If you'd like, sprinkle the shakshuka with crumbled feta cheese.

Garnish with fresh parsley.

Serve the shakshuka warm, ideally with a side of crusty bread for dipping.

Mum and the Therapist

A young man goes to see his psychotherapist.

"You know, I had the weirdest dream. I was talking to my mother, but she had your face. I was so agitated and freaked out that I couldn't get back to sleep. I tossed and turned all night.

Finally, I got up at six o'clock, made myself some toast and a coffee, and then came straight here. What do you think the dream means?"

The therapist pondered for a moment and then says, "A slice of toast and some coffee? You call that a breakfast?"

Matzo Brei

Matzo Brei, often dubbed "Passover's French Toast," is a culinary chameleon? Originating from the Ashkenazi Jewish tradition, it's made from matzo broken into pieces and soaked in water or milk, then fried with eggs. Depending on personal or family preferences, Matzo Brei can swing either sweet or savory! Some folks drizzle it with syrup or sprinkle it with sugar, while others add salt, pepper, or even sautéed onions.

Ingredients:

4 sheets of matzo
4 large eggs
Salt to taste
2 tablespoons unsalted butter or oil
Optional: sugar, cinnamon, maple syrup, or preserves for a sweet version; or onions, garlic, and pepper for a savory version

Instructions:

Break the matzo into pieces and place them in a large bowl.
Cover the matzo with hot water or milk and let it sit for about a minute to soften. Then drain the water from the bowl.
In a separate bowl, beat the eggs and add salt to taste.
Add the beaten eggs to the drained matzo and mix well.
Heat the butter or oil in a large skillet over medium heat.
Pour the matzo and egg mixture into the skillet. Cook until the bottom is golden brown, about 3-5 minutes.
Flip the matzo brei over and cook the other side until it's also golden brown, about another 3-5 minutes. You can do this either by flipping it as a whole like a pancake or by breaking it up and stirring it like scrambled eggs, depending on your preference.
Serve the matzo brei warm. If you prefer a sweet version, sprinkle it with sugar and cinnamon or serve it with maple syrup or preserves. If you prefer a savoury version, you can add sautéed onions, garlic, and pepper before cooking.

Chutzpah

As the holiday flight landed and taxied to its stand at Ben Gurion airport, the Captain announced:

"Welcome to Israel! Please remain seated with your seatbelt fastened until our plane comes to a complete stop. I repeat, do not stand up until the seat belt signs have been turned off."

"For those of you still in your seats, we wish you a very Merry Christmas! For those standing in the aisles, Happy Hanukkah!"

Simple Salt Beef Recipe

Salt beef, also known as corned beef in some regions, has its origins steeped in preservation necessity. Despite its name "salt beef," the dish is often boiled, which dilutes some of the saltiness. Paired with mustard or pickles on a sandwich, it's the comeback story of a super-salty meat turned deli superstar!

Ingredients:

2.25 kg beef brisket or silverside
4 cups water
1/2 cup kosher salt
1/4 cup brown sugar or granulated sugar
1/4 cup crushed black peppercorns
5 cloves garlic, minced
2 tablespoons curing salt (pink salt or Prague powder #1) - optional, but this gives the beef its traditional pink color
3 bay leaves, crushed
1 tablespoon mustard seeds
1 tablespoon coriander seeds
1 teaspoon juniper berries, crushed (optional)
1 teaspoon thyme, dried
1 teaspoon allspice berries (optional)

Instructions:

In a large pot, combine water, kosher salt, sugar, crushed black peppercorns, garlic, curing salt (if using), and all other spices.

Heat the mixture over medium heat and stir until the salt and sugar are completely dissolved.

Remove from heat and let it cool to room temperature.

Then refrigerate until chilled.

While the brine is cooling, trim the beef brisket of any excess fat, but leave a thin layer to keep the meat moist during cooking.

Once the brine is chilled, place the beef brisket in a large, non-reactive container (like a glass or ceramic dish) or a large resealable plastic bag.

Pour the brine over the beef, ensuring it's fully submerged. If using a plastic bag, remove as much air as possible and seal it.

Place the container or bag in the refrigerator.

Brine the beef for at least 5-7 days, turning the meat once a day to ensure even brining.

Cooking the Salt Beef

After brining, remove the beef from the brine and rinse it thoroughly under cold running water.

Place the beef in a large pot and cover with water.

Bring to a boil, then reduce the heat to low, cover, and simmer for about 3-4 hours or until the beef is tender.

Add a variety of vegetables to boost the flavour and enjoyment of this special recipe.

The Rabbi Who Played Golf on Yom Kippur

A rabbi was so addicted to golf that he decided to sneak out to play a round between the morning and afternoon services on Yom Kippur.

Up in Heaven, Moses turned to G-d and said, "What a disgrace. Not just a Jew playing golf on Yom Kippur, but a rabbi!". The Almighty responded, "I'll teach him a lesson."

Out on the course, where the rabbi had been playing reasonably well, he stepped up to the seventh tee and drove his ball down the fairway. His ball bounced off a sprinkler head, hit a tree, a bunker rake, rolled onto the green and straight into the cup.

"This is how You teach him a lesson, Lord? He got a hole in one!"
"Sure, but who's he going to tell?"

Simple Falafel

Falafel is a popular Middle Eastern dish made from ground chickpeas or fava beans, mixed with herbs and spices, then formed into small balls or patties and deep-fried until crispy. Falafel is often served in pita bread with tahini sauce, salad, and pickles, making them a widely loved vegetarian street food.

Ingredients:

2 cups dried chickpeas (do not use canned chickpeas)
1 small onion, roughly chopped
3-4 garlic cloves, minced
1/4 cup fresh parsley, chopped
1/4 cup fresh cilantro, chopped (optional)
1 tablespoon ground cumin
1 teaspoon ground coriander
1/4 teaspoon chili powder or cayenne pepper (adjust to preference)
1 teaspoon baking powder
Salt to taste
Oil for frying

Instructions:

Place dried chickpeas in a large bowl and cover with cold water. Allow them to soak overnight, or at least 12 hours. They will double in size.
Drain and rinse the soaked chickpeas. In a food processor, combine chickpeas, onions, garlic, parsley, cilantro, cumin, coriander, chili powder/cayenne pepper, and salt. Process until you get a smooth paste-like consistency but not too smooth; it should still have a slightly grainy texture.
Transfer the mixture to a bowl and stir in the baking powder.
Using your hands or a falafel scoop, form the mixture into small balls or patties.
In a deep-frying pan, heat the oil over medium heat. Once hot, carefully fry the falafel balls/patties in batches, making sure not to overcrowd the pan. Fry until golden brown on each side, about 3-5 minutes per side.
Once fried, remove falafels with a slotted spoon and let them drain on paper towels. Serve them hot with tahini sauce, in pita pockets, and/or with salads and pickles.

The Praying Parrot

Yankel bought a parrot, hoping to teach it to say a few words. The next morning, he found the bird on the eastern side of its cage, rocking back and forth, mumbling. Stooping to listen, Yankel was shocked to hear his new parrot praying, in Hebrew.

"You're Jewish?!"

"Of course. Modern Orthodox. Are we going to shul on Rosh Hashanah?"

"You want me to take you to synagogue?! This is unbelievable. Is this a secret? Can I tell my friends about you?"

"Tell anyone you want. Now let me finish davening."

Yankel immediately started bragging about his Jewish parrot. Of course, no one believed him, so he started taking bets. By Rosh Hashanah he had two thousand pounds riding on the bird.

On the Day of Judgement, Yankel proudly set his parrot in front of the room. Everyone stared, even the rabbi, who bet fifty pounds against the parrot praying.

Yankel urged it to pray. People started to laugh. The parrot clucked a few times but it didn't pray. Yankel begged, but still the parrot stayed silent. Yankel lost the two thousand pounds.

Back at home, Yankel grabbed the parrot by its scrawny neck. "Now you better start praying. You humiliated me! You're a dead bird!"

"Don't be a schmuck, Yankel! Yom Kippur's next week. Everyone looks forward all year to the cantor singing Kol Nidrei on Yom Kippur. Tell everyone I'll be singing Kol Nidrei."

"Why would I do that?! You didn't even pray in shul today!" "Exactly," said the parrot, "think of the odds we'll get!"

Israeli-Style Fish Cakes

Israeli-Style Fish Cakes are a delightful dish that draw on the diverse culinary tapestry of the region. While fish cakes might seem universally straightforward, the Israeli twist often incorporates a medley of spices like cumin, coriander, and turmeric.

Ingredients:

450g mixed fish filets (such as cod, haddock, or sea bass), boneless and skinless
1 large onion, finely chopped
2 garlic cloves, minced
1/4 cup fresh cilantro, chopped and 1/4 cup fresh parsley, chopped
1-2 fresh green chilies (adjust to your heat preference), deseeded and finely chopped
2 large eggs
1/4 cup breadcrumbs or matzah meal
1 teaspoon ground cumin and ground cumin
Salt and pepper to taste
Oil for frying (like olive oil or vegetable oil)

For the Sauce:

1 can (14 oz) diced tomatoes
2 garlic cloves, minced
1 teaspoon ground cumin and 1/2 teaspoon ground paprika
Salt and pepper to taste
1 tablespoon olive oil

Instructions:

In a food processor, combine fish filets, chopped onion, garlic, cilantro, parsley, green chilies, eggs, breadcrumbs or matzah meal, cumin, paprika, salt, and pepper. Process until the mixture becomes a coarse paste.

With wet hands, shape the fish mixture into small patties.

Heat oil in a large skillet over medium heat.

Fry the patties in batches, ensuring they're golden brown on both sides.

Once fried, set them aside on a plate lined with paper towels.

In the same skillet, add a bit more oil if necessary. Sauté minced garlic until fragrant.

Add diced tomatoes, cumin, paprika, salt, and pepper.

Let the sauce simmer for about 10 minutes until it thickens slightly.

Gently place the fried fish cakes into the tomato sauce, letting them simmer for another 5-7 minutes so they can soak up some of the sauce.

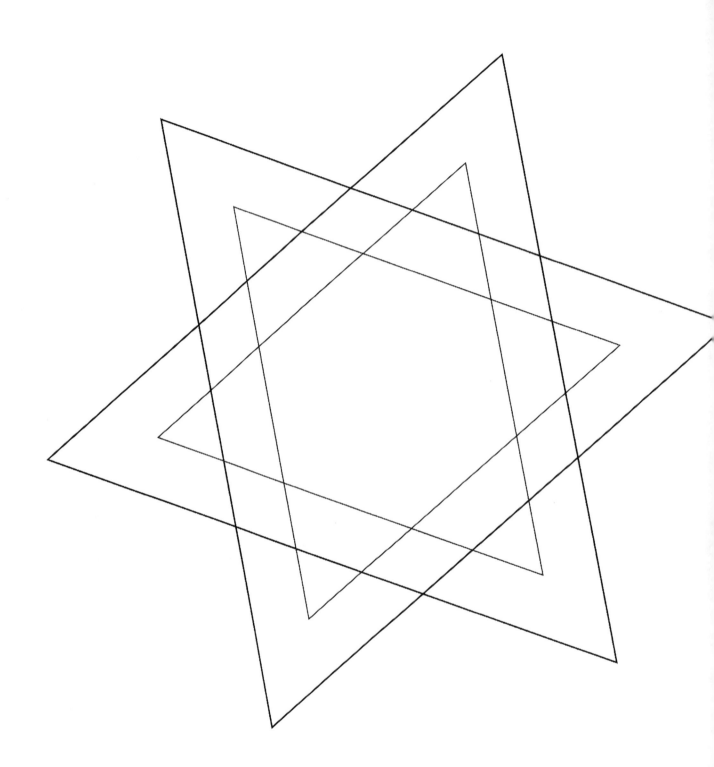

Who Said My Father Died?

Yitzy visits his doctor for his annual check-up. "Yitzy, you're in terrific shape for a 60-year-old. You have the body of a 35-year-old. Tell me, how old was your father when he died?"

"Who said my father died?"
"Wow! How old is he, and is he active?"
"Dad's 82, he runs or cycles three times a week."
"Amazing! How old was your grandfather when he died?"
"Who said my grandfather died?"
"You're kidding. How old is he, and is he active?"
"Grandpa is 102, still runs and cycles, and he's about to get married again."
"Wow! But why on earth would a 102-year-old want to get married again?"
"Who said he wanted to? His mother pressured him into it!"

Savoury Potato Kugel

Savoury Potato Kugel is like the ultimate Jewish answer to hash browns, with its crisp exterior and fluffy interior. In old Ashkenazi Jewish communities, before the widespread availability of ovens, kugels were often slow cooked overnight in communal bakeries.

As families would finish their Friday evening meals, they'd drop off their potato kugel to bake in the residual heat of the baker's oven, retrieving it the next day, piping hot for Shabbat lunch.

So, every bite of this dish is not just full of potato goodness, but also carries with it a tradition of community and togetherness!

Ingredients for Savoury Potato Kugel:

5 large potatoes, peeled and grated
1 large onion, finely chopped or grated
3 large eggs, beaten
1/3 cup (40g) all-purpose flour or matzah meal
1 teaspoon salt
1/2 teaspoon black pepper
1/4 cup (60ml) vegetable oil or schmaltz (chicken fat)

Instructions for Savoury Potato Kugel:

Preheat the oven to 190°C/375°F and grease a 23 x 33 cm baking dish.

After grating the potatoes, place them in a clean kitchen towel and wring out any excess moisture.

In a large bowl, combine the potatoes, onion, eggs, flour or matzo meal, salt, and pepper.

Heat the oil or schmaltz in the oven in the baking dish until it's hot. Carefully remove from the oven and pour the potato mixture into the hot oil.

Spread the mixture evenly in the dish and bake for about 45-55 minutes, or until the kugel is crispy on top and set.

Allow to cool slightly before serving.

Savoury kugel is especially good with roasted meats.

The Two Jews

Two elderly Jewish men went out for a walk, when suddenly it began to rain.

"Quick," said Abe, "open your umbrella."

"It won't help," said Izzy. "My umbrella is full of holes."

"Then why did you bring it?"

"I didn't think it would rain!"

Jewish Style Briskets

Jewish-style brisket is a classic dish often associated with Ashkenazi Jewish traditions, particularly during holidays like Passover, Rosh Hashanah, and Hanukkah. The slow-cooked nature of the dish results in a tender, flavorful meat, often accompanied by a rich sauce or gravy. Here's a basic recipe for Jewish-style brisket:

Ingredients:

Brisket - about 1.8 - 2.25Kgs
2 large onions, sliced
4 cloves garlic, minced
2 cups beef or chicken broth
1 cup red wine (or you can use additional broth)
2 tablespoons tomato paste
2 tablespoons vegetable oil or schmaltz
2 bay leaves
1 teaspoon dried thyme or a couple of sprigs of fresh thyme
Salt and pepper to taste

Instructions:

Generously season both sides of the brisket with salt and pepper.

Allow it to come to room temperature for about an hour. In a large oven-proof pot or Dutch oven, heat the oil or schmaltz over medium-high heat.

Once hot, add the brisket (fat side down) and brown for about 4-5 minutes on each side. Remove the brisket from the pot and set aside.

In the same pot, add the sliced onions. Sauté until they begin to caramelize, then add the garlic and cook for another 1-2 minutes.

Stir in the tomato paste and cook for a minute. Then, pour in the red wine, scraping the bottom of the pan to release any browned bits. Allow the wine to simmer and reduce by half.

Then, add the beef or chicken broth.

Place the brisket back into the pot, fatty side up. Add the bay leaves and thyme.

The liquid should come about halfway up the side of the brisket.

Preheat your oven to 165°C / 325°F. Cover the pot with a tight-fitting lid or foil.

Transfer the pot to the oven and braise for about 3-4 hours, turning the brisket halfway through cooking.

If you want to add carrots and potatoes, put them in during the last hour of cooking.

Once the brisket is fork-tender, remove it from the oven.

Let it rest for about 15-20 minutes before slicing against the grain.

Serve: Strain the cooking liquid and serve it as a gravy alongside the brisket slices.

Directions in the Old City

A Jewish American tourist is strolling through the Old City of Jerusalem and approaches a local Hasidic Israeli. "Excuse me, how long will it take me to walk to the Western Wall?"

The Israeli ignores him. "Excuse me, how long will it take me to get the Wall from here?"

Again, the Israeli doesn't answer.

The American asks again in Hebrew, but still the Israeli doesn't answer.

"I don't understand why you Hasidim won't accept me! I'm your fellow Jew.

The American turns and walks away. A minute later the Israeli runs up behind him and says, "It'll take you eight minutes from here."

"Why are you telling me now?"

"I didn't know how fast you walk."

Chicken Schnitzel

Chicken schnitzel is a popular dish in many countries and has been readily adopted and enjoyed in Israel and among Jewish communities worldwide, often becoming a staple in many households. The dish involves thinly pounded chicken breasts that are breaded and fried until golden and crispy.

Ingredients:

4 boneless, skinless chicken breasts
1 cup all-purpose flour
2 large eggs, beaten
2 cups breadcrumbs (traditional or panko for extra crispiness)
2 teaspoons salt, divided
1 teaspoon black pepper
Optional: 1 teaspoon paprika or garlic powder for added flavor in the breadcrumbs
Vegetable oil for frying
Lemon wedges for serving

Instructions:

Place a chicken breast between two pieces of plastic wrap or parchment paper. Using a meat mallet, rolling pin, or the flat side of a heavy knife, pound the chicken until it is about 0.5-0.75cm thick. Repeat with the remaining chicken breasts.
In one shallow dish, mix the flour with 1 teaspoon of salt. In a separate dish, beat the eggs. In a third dish, mix the breadcrumbs with the remaining 1 teaspoon of salt, black pepper, and any optional seasonings like paprika or garlic powder. Coat each chicken breast in the flour mixture, shaking off any excess. Dip into the beaten eggs, ensuring it's fully coated. Finally, press the chicken into the breadcrumbs, ensuring it's evenly and fully coated.
In a large frying pan, heat about 0.5cm of vegetable oil over medium heat. Once the oil is hot, add the breaded chicken. Fry for about 3-4 minutes on each side or until golden brown and cooked through. You might need to fry in batches to avoid overcrowding the pan.
Remove the schnitzel from the pan and place them on a plate lined with paper towels to drain any excess oil. Serve hot with lemon wedges.

Two Synagogues

A Jewish man is shipwrecked on a desert island where he ends up being stuck for years and years. Using materials from around the island, he builds a house, a shop, and a synagogue.

Eventually, he's constructed an entire neighborhood. One day, he's rescued by a passing ship.

The sailors help him collect his few possessions and they get ready to leave the island forever.

Just before they leave, one of the sailors says,

"Hey, why did you build two synagogues?"

The man rolls his eyes.

"This," he says, pointing at one building, "is my synagogue."

"And that," he says, pointing at the other, "is the one I would never set foot in!"

Classic Cream Cheese & Smoked Salmon Bagel

The combination of smoked salmon and cream cheese on a bagel is a quintessential Jewish delicacy, especially popular within the Ashkenazi Jewish community.

It's regularly enjoyed during breakfast or brunch, but it's delicious any time of the day. Here's how to assemble a classic Jewish smoked salmon and cream cheese bagel:

Ingredients:

1 bagel
2-3 oz smoked salmon
2 tablespoons cream cheese (or more, to taste)
Thinly sliced red onion (optional)
Thinly sliced cucumber (optional, for crunch)
Fresh dill (for garnish)
Lemon wedges
Tomato slices (optional)
Black pepper (optional)

Instructions:

Oven warm your bagel or, slice the bagel in half and toast it to your desired level.

Some prefer it lightly toasted to retain the bagel's chewy interior, while others like it crispier.

Once toasted, while the bagel is still warm, generously spread cream cheese on each half.

Layer the smoked salmon on top of the cream cheese. Be generous as you like!

If using, place the thinly sliced red onion, cucumber, and tomato slices on top of the smoked salmon.

Add a sprinkle of black pepper and a squeeze of lemon juice. Garnish with fresh dill if you'd like.

Enjoy your classic Jewish smoked salmon and cream cheese bagel with a side of pickles or coleslaw, and perhaps a cup of coffee for a perfect meal!

Playing Poker

A rabbi, a priest, and a minister are playing poker in the back room of a cafe when the police raid the game.

The officer in charge questions the priest,

"Father Patrick, were you gambling?"

Father Patrick silently asks G-d to forgive him for the lie he's about to tell.

"No, Officer. I was not gambling."

The officer turns to the minister,

"Pastor Murphy, were you gambling?"

Pastor Murphy also makes his appeal to the heavens, turns to the policeman and says, "No, officer, I was not gambling."

The policeman finally turns to the rabbi. "Rabbi Goldstein, were you gambling?"

"Gambling?" he asks, glancing at the priest and the minister, "with who?"

Baked Salmon with Herb Tahini Sauce

Baked salmon with an herb tahini sauce combines the rich, buttery flavor of the fish with the nutty, herbaceous kick of the tahini. This is a straightforward recipe that infuses Middle Eastern flavors into a classic salmon dish.

Baked Salmon Ingredients:

4 salmon filets
2 tablespoons olive oil
Salt and pepper to taste
1 lemon, zested and juiced
2 cloves garlic, minced

Ingredients for Herb Tahini Sauce:

1/2 cup tahini
1/4 cup water (or more for desired consistency)
2 tablespoons lemon juice
2 tablespoons olive oil
1 small clove garlic, minced
1/4 cup chopped fresh parsley
1/4 cup chopped fresh cilantro (optional)
Salt and pepper to taste
1-2 tablespoons honey or maple syrup (optional, for sweetness)
A pinch of red pepper flakes or cayenne for a little heat (optional)

Instructions to Bake the Salmon:

Preheat your oven to 200°C / 400°F.
Place salmon filets skin-side down in a baking dish.

Rub each filet with olive oil, minced garlic, lemon zest, and lemon juice. Season with salt and pepper.

Bake in the preheated oven for 12-15 minutes or until salmon flakes easily with a fork. The cooking time might vary based on the thickness of the filets.

Prepare the Herb Tahini Sauce:

In a bowl, whisk together the tahini, water, lemon juice, olive oil, and minced garlic until smooth.

The sauce should be creamy but pourable, so adjust with more water if necessary.

Stir in the chopped parsley and cilantro. Season with salt and pepper.

Taste and adjust the flavour.

If you'd like a bit of sweetness to counteract the bitterness of tahini, add honey or maple syrup.

If you prefer a bit of heat, add red pepper flakes or cayenne.

Serve: Once the salmon is cooked, plate each filet, and generously drizzle with the herb tahini sauce.

Garnish with additional fresh herbs or lemon wedges if desired.

Jewish Grandfather

A Jewish grandfather takes his grandchildren to the beach.

They're playing in the sand when suddenly, a huge wave comes and pulls the smallest grandson out into the water.

Panicked, the grandfather prays to G-d.

"Oh G-d, please bring him back! Please let him live!"

Suddenly, an even bigger wave bursts out of the ocean, setting the little boy down right at his grandfather's feet.

He scoops him up into a hug.

Then he stares up to heaven and says,

"He had a hat."

DESERTS

Cheese Blintzes with Cherry Topping

These rolled filled pancakes are yet another dish of Ashkenazi Jewish origin.

Ingredients for the Blintzes:

1 cup all-purpose flour
1.5 cups milk
2 eggs
2 tablespoons melted butter
Pinch of salt
Additional butter for frying

Instructions:

In a blender, combine the flour, milk, eggs, melted butter, and salt.

Blend until smooth. Let the batter rest for about 30 minutes to allow the flour to fully absorb the liquid.

Heat a non-stick pan over medium heat and lightly brush with butter.

Pour a small amount of batter into the pan, swirling to cover the bottom in a thin layer.

Cook until the edges begin to lightly brown, then flip and cook for an additional 30 seconds. Transfer to a plate and repeat with the remaining batter. Set the crepes aside.

Ingredients for the Cheese Filling:

1.5 cups cottage or ricotta cheese
1/4 cup cream cheese, softened
1/4 cup granulated sugar

1 large egg yolk
1 teaspoon vanilla extract
Zest of 1 lemon

Instructions:

In a mixing bowl, combine all the filling ingredients. Mix until smooth and fully combined.

Ingredients for the Cherry Topping:

2 cups fresh or frozen cherries, pitted
1/4 cup granulated sugar
1/2 cup water
1 tablespoon corn flour (dissolved in 2 tablespoons cold water)
1 teaspoon lemon juice

Instructions:

In a saucepan, combine cherries, sugar, and water. Bring to a simmer.

Once the cherries are soft and the liquid is slightly reduced, add the corn flour mixture. Stir constantly until the sauce thickens. Remove from heat and add lemon juice.

Assembling and Cooking the Blintzes:

Place a crepe, browned side up, on a work surface. Place a spoonful of the cheese mixture in the center.

Fold the bottom edge over the filling, then fold in the sides, and then roll it up to fully enclose the filling.

In a pan, melt some butter over medium heat.

Place the blintzes seam-side down and cook until golden brown on both sides.

Serve the blintzes warm, topped with the cherry sauce.

Jewish Grandmother

A Jewish grandmother is giving directions to her adult grandson who is coming to visit with his wife.

"You come to the front door of the apartments. I am in apartment 301. There is a big panel at the front door. With your elbow, push button 301. I'll buzz you in. Come inside and the lift is on the right. Get in, and with your elbow, push 3rd Floor. When you get out, I'm on the left. With your elbow, hit my doorbell. OK?"

"Grandma, that sounds easy, but why am I hitting all these buttons with my elbow?"

"What... you're coming empty handed?"

Chocolate Babka Cake

Originating from Eastern Europe, Chocolate Babka Cake is an irresistible sweet bread swirled with rich chocolate. One theory of its Jewish origins is that it is thought to have come about during the early 1800s.

Housewives making dough for challah bread would have prepared extra dough, to be filled with cinnamon or jam (or in this case chocolate), which was then rolled up and baked as a special treat.

Dough Ingredients:

1/2 cup whole milk, lukewarm
2 teaspoons active dry yeast
1/4 cup granulated sugar
4 cups all-purpose flour, more for dusting
1/2 teaspoon salt
1 teaspoon vanilla extract
3 large eggs, beaten
1/2 cup unsalted butter, softened

Chocolate Filling Ingredients:

3/4 cup semi-sweet chocolate chips or coarsely chopped chocolate
1/2 cup unsalted butter
1/2 cup powdered sugar
1/3 cup unsweetened cocoa powder
1/4 teaspoon cinnamon (optional)

Syrup Ingredients (for glazing):

1/2 cup water

1/2 cup granulated sugar

Instructions for Dough Preparation:

In a small bowl, combine lukewarm milk, 1 tablespoon of sugar, and yeast. Allow to sit for about 10 minutes until frothy. In a large bowl or the bowl of a stand mixer, combine the flour, remaining sugar, and salt. Add the yeast mixture, beaten eggs, and vanilla. Mix until a sticky dough forms.
Add the softened butter, one piece at a time, until incorporated. Knead the dough for about 10 minutes, either by hand on a floured surface or with a dough hook in a stand mixer, until smooth and elastic. Place the dough in a greased bowl, cover, and let rise in a warm place for 1-1.5 hours, or until doubled in size.

Instructions for Chocolate Filling:

In a saucepan, melt the butter and chocolate, stirring until smooth. Remove from heat and stir in powdered sugar, cocoa powder, and cinnamon, if using.

Assembling the Babka:

Roll out the risen dough on a floured surface into a rectangle, about 1/4 inch thick. Spread the chocolate filling over the dough, leaving a small border around the edges. Roll the dough into a log, lengthwise. Cut the log in half down the middle, lengthwise, so you have two long halves with layers of dough and filling exposed.
Twist the two halves around each other, creating a braid. Transfer the braided dough to a greased loaf pan. Let the babka rise again for about 45 minutes to 1 hour.

Baking & Syrup:

Preheat your oven to 190°C/375°F. Bake the babka for about 25-30 minutes or until golden brown.
While the babka is baking, make the syrup by combining sugar and water in a small saucepan. Bring to a simmer and cook until the sugar dissolves. Remove from heat. As soon as the babka comes out of the oven, brush it generously with the sugar syrup to give it a glossy finish and to keep it moist.
Cool & Serve: Allow the babka to cool in the loaf pan for about 10-15 minutes, then transfer to a wire rack to cool completely before slicing.

Bubaleh

A young Jewish Mother walks her son to the school bus on his first day of kindergarten.

"Behave, my bubaleh," she says.

"Take good care of yourself and think about your Mother, tataleh!"

"And come right back home on the bus, schein kindaleh."

"Your Mommy loves you a lot, my ketsaleh!"

At the end of the school day the bus comes back, and she runs to her son and hugs him.

"So, what did my pupaleh learn on his first day of school?"

The boy answers,

"I learned my name is Daniel."

Jewish Apple Cake

Jewish Apple Cake is a moist and flavourful cake that's traditionally made during the Jewish High Holidays, particularly Rosh Hashanah, when eating apples dipped in honey symbolizes the wish for a sweet new year. It is typically dairy-free, which means it can be eaten after a meat meal according to kosher dietary laws.

Ingredients:

5 medium-sized apples, peeled, cored, and sliced (Granny Smith or Golden Delicious work well)
2 teaspoons cinnamon
3 tablespoons granulated sugar
2 3/4 cups all-purpose flour
1 tablespoon baking powder
1 teaspoon salt
2 cups granulated sugar
1 cup vegetable oil
1/4 cup orange juice
2 1/2 teaspoons vanilla extract
4 large eggs

Instructions:

In a large bowl, toss the apple slices with cinnamon and sugar. Set aside.

Preheat your oven to 175°C/350°F. Grease a tube or Bundt tin.

In a medium-sized bowl, sift together the flour, baking powder, and salt. Set aside.

In a large bowl, whisk together the sugar, oil, orange juice, and vanilla extract. Add the eggs one at a time, whisking well after each addition.

Gradually add the dry ingredients to the wet ingredients, mixing just until combined.

Pour one-third of the batter into the prepared pan.

Layer half of the apples on top.

Pour another one-third of the batter over the apples.

Layer the remaining apples on top.

Pour the remaining batter over the apples, ensuring they're covered.

Place the pan in the preheated oven and bake for about 60-75 minutes, or until a toothpick inserted into the center of the cake comes out clean.

If the cake is browning too quickly, you can cover it loosely with aluminium foil.

Once baked, remove the cake from the oven and let it cool in the pan for about 15 minutes. Then, invert the cake onto a wire rack and allow it to cool completely.

Once cooled, you can optionally dust the cake with powdered sugar for presentation.

The Yom Kippur Ticket

A boy shows up at synagogue on Yom Kippur without a ticket and the usher won't let him in.

"Listen, I'm not staying,' says the boy, "I just need to talk to my mother!"

"Okay," the usher says, "but if I catch you praying, you're out!"

Honey Cake

Jewish Honey Cake, or 'lekach', is another traditional Ashkenazi dish. Traditionally eaten during Rosh Hashanah, the honey symbolizes the wish for a sweet year ahead.

Ingredients:

3 1/2 cups all-purpose flour
1 tablespoon baking powder
1 teaspoon baking soda
1/2 teaspoon salt
4 teaspoons ground cinnamon
1/2 teaspoon ground cloves
1/2 teaspoon ground allspice
1 cup vegetable oil
1 cup honey
1 1/2 cups granulated sugar
1/2 cup brown sugar
3 large eggs
1 teaspoon vanilla extract
1 cup warm coffee or strong tea
1/2 cup fresh orange juice
1/2 cup slivered or chopped almonds (optional)

Instructions:

Preheat oven to 175°C / 350°F. Grease a 23 x 33cm cake pan or two round pans.

In a large bowl, whisk together the flour, baking powder, baking soda, salt, cinnamon, cloves, and allspice. Set aside.

In another bowl, whisk together the oil, honey, granulated sugar, brown sugar, eggs, and vanilla extract.

Mix until smooth. Make a well in the centre of the dry ingredients.

Add the wet mixture to the dry, alternating with the coffee (or tea) and orange juice.

Ensure everything is combined well but avoid over-mixing.

Fold in the slivered or chopped almonds if you're using them.

Pour the batter into the prepared pan(s). If using a rectangular baking tin, bake for 40 minutes.

If using round tins, bake for 30 minutes. If using a Bundt tin, it might take up to 60 minutes.

A toothpick inserted into the center should come out with a few crumbs attached, but not wet.

Remove from the oven and let the cake cool in the pan for about 15 minutes.

Then, invert onto a wire rack and let it cool completely.

You can drizzle with additional honey or dust with powdered sugar before serving if desired.

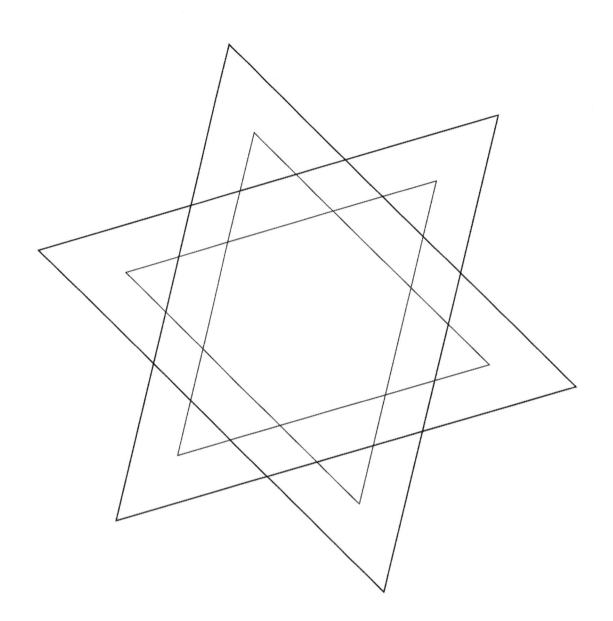

The Haircut

On the Shabbat before Passover, Rabbi Levi is delivering his most important sermon of the year. In the middle of his lesson, Ezra gets up and walks out of the synagogue.

The next day, Rabbi Levi sees Ezra on the street.

"Ezra, wait a second."

"Morning, Rabbi."

"Ezra, why did you walk out during my sermon yesterday?"

"I needed a haircut."

"Why didn't you get your haircut before my sermon?"

"I didn't need one."

Sweet Kugel

Kugel is another traditional Ashkenazi Jewish dish, often made from noodles or potatoes. It's often described as a baked pudding and typically served on Shabbat or Jewish holidays.

While savoury kugels are also quite popular, the sweet varieties, often containing ingredients like cinnamon, raisins, or apples, are like a delicious crossover between a dessert and a side dish.

Ingredients

450g wide egg noodles
1/2 cup (115g) unsalted butter, melted
1 cup (240ml) sour cream
1 cup (240ml) cottage cheese
1 cup (200g) granulated sugar
6 large eggs
1 teaspoon vanilla extract
1/2 teaspoon ground cinnamon
1/2 cup raisins (optional)

Instructions

Preheat the oven to 175°C/350°F and grease a 23x33cm baking dish.
Cook the noodles according to package instructions, then drain.
In a large bowl, combine melted butter, sour cream, cottage cheese, sugar, eggs, vanilla, and cinnamon. Stir in the cooked noodles and raisins, if using.
Pour the mixture into the prepared dish.
Bake for about 50-60 minutes or until the kugel is set and the top is golden brown.
Allow to cool slightly before serving. Sprinkle with additional cinnamon or sugar if desired.

The Debate

Four rabbis were having a debate about a crucial matter regarding Jewish law. Each stated their case and then voted. It was three to one against Rabbi Hoffman.

But Rabbi Hoffman knew he was right! He cried out to heaven, "G-d, please send a sign to prove that I am right."

Out of a clear sky, it suddenly began to snow. Rabbi Hoffman said, "You see!" One of the other rabbis says, "It's snowing in winter. You call that a sign?"

Rabbi Hoffman said, "G-d please, make it a clearer sign." Suddenly out of the sky, a lightning strike splits a tree in half. Rabbi Hoffman cried, "It's a miracle!" The second rabbi said, "Lightning from the sky. This you call a miracle?"

Before Rabbi Hoffman could appeal to G-d one more time, the sky darkened and a booming voice called out from heaven, "The law is according to Rabbi Hoffman."

Hoffman says, "There, now you see."

The third rabbi says, "Meh. So now it's three to two."

Sufganiyot

Sufganiyot are deep-fried doughnuts, referencing the miracle of the oil that lasted eight days in the Hanukkah story. Every year around Hanukkah, many Jewish bakeries engage in friendly competition, trying to outdo each other with unique and delicious fillings, from classic jelly to creme Brulee and even savoury options.

Ingredients:

2 tablespoons active dry yeast
1/2 cup warm water
1/4 cup plus 1 teaspoon sugar, divided
2 1/2 cups all-purpose flour
2 large eggs
2 tablespoons unsalted butter, room temperature
1/2 teaspoon freshly grated nutmeg
2 teaspoons salt
3 cups vegetable oil, plus more for a bowl
1 cup seedless raspberry jam

Instructions:

In a small bowl, combine yeast, warm water, and 1 teaspoon of sugar. Set aside until foamy, about 10 minutes.

Place flour in a large bowl. Make a well in the centre; add eggs, yeast mixture, 1/4 cup sugar, butter, nutmeg, and salt. Using a spoon, stir until a sticky dough forms.

On a well-floured surface, knead until dough is smooth, elastic, and bounces back when poked with a finger, about 8 minutes (add more flour, as needed).

Place in an oiled bowl; cover with plastic wrap. Set in a warm place to rise until doubled, 1 to 1 1/2 hours.

On a lightly floured surface, roll the dough to approx. 0.5cm thickness.

Using a 6.5cm round cutter or drinking glass, cut 20 rounds. Cover with plastic wrap; let rise for 15 minutes.

In a medium saucepan over medium heat, heat oil until a deep-frying thermometer registering 180°C.

Using a slotted spoon, carefully slip 4 rounds into the oil.

Fry until golden, about 40 seconds.

Turn doughnuts over; fry until golden on the other side, another 40 seconds.

Using a slotted spoon, transfer to a paper-towel-lined baking sheet.

Fill a pastry bag fitted with 4 tips with jam.

Using a wooden skewer or toothpick, make a hole in the side of each doughnut.

Fit the pastry tip into a hole, and pipe about 2 teaspoons of jam into the doughnut.

Repeat with remaining doughnuts.

Ezra's Final Wish

Old Jacob is lying on his deathbed with his grandson Gideon by his side.

Jacob turns to the boy, "Go down and get some of your grandmother's rugelach from the kitchen, so that should be the very last thing I taste in this world."

Three minutes later, Gideon returns empty handed.

Jacob asks, "Where's the rugelach?"

The grandson replies, "Bubbe says she's saving it for the shiva."

Printed in Great Britain
by Amazon